The Cavalcade

poems by

July Westhale

Finishing Line Press
Georgetown, Kentucky

The Cavalcade

ACKNOWLEDGMENTS

"If V. Woolf filled her pockets with balloons instead of rocks" first appeared in
burntdistrict.
"After Time Has Rumpled the Sheets of Your Mouth" first appeared in *Barely
South Review*.
"V. Woolf Printing Ulysses", "Alternative Bedtime Story" (under the name
"Canopy"), and "To the larks, who know nothing of what we do," were published
in the 2014 issue of *Adrienne*.
"Ars Poetica" (under the name "The Last Five Years") appeared in *The Tahoma
Review*, and was printed as a broadside by Damask Press.
"Dirty War" first appeared in *Shadow Graph*.
"Intolerable Objects/Tomato" first appeared in *Sweet Wolverine*.
"Freud Looking at a Picture of His Mother" is forthcoming from
cahoodaloodaling.

Publisher: Leah Maines

Editor: Christen Kincaid

Cover Art: Pamela Petro

Author Photo: Elizabeth C. Ehrenpreis

Cover Design: Elizabeth Maines

Printed in the USA on acid-free paper.
Order online: www.finishinglinepress.com
also available on amazon.com

Author inquiries and mail orders:
Finishing Line Press
P. O. Box 1626
Georgetown, Kentucky 40324
U. S. A.

Table of Contents

I. *Brightly Human*

II. *Millions, Myriads*

I. Brightly Human

"Throw over your man…and I'll tell you all the things I have in my head, millions, myriads,"

—letter from Virginia Woolf to Vita Sackville-West, 1927

Mean Landscapes

The heavens opened up.
        The rain was sad, and drowned itself

we didn't know there would
be no going back
        (the way we came)—

How could we
know this landscape made mean

        with want, with a crescent of wet
        on a desert skyline? Our bodies are parched.
        The cacti are chubby like engorged hearts.

Yet…what did we know of desert?
A thin line of heartbeat,
the road a long, dark, shadow.

        You lucky girls. You made landscape
        break apart and drown.

Writing the Canon

We had been taught to sit still, when asked
for the salt, the pepper, the brandy, the knife.
To cut small, and eat smaller. To be as such—
eyes follow in the street. To speak
softly, and commit trespasses of faintness.

                                        To be nothing
but a thumbprint on a pages of words.
There are none of us here. We've died.

When we haven't, we've suffered
worse—a small blip on memory's seismograph,
an unfathomable, frantic set of lines,

                                    gone red red red.

Poem in Which I Rewrite History

Every Sunday, we think about driving to church,
but instead end up fucking

execution style: gruesomely, and against a wall.
I get caught in the headlights

of our love, and moon about intersections
like a lost traffic cone, orange and useless.

It's always the same ending: our streets
slick and blurry in the spectacular light of accidents,

like arctic borealis. I ask far too much:
to be a destination where I might crash and wreck.

In reality, we are earnest

with our destruction, truthful

as a salt-eaten screen door, and as loud.

Donner Pass, 2012

> *"May we with Gods help spend the comeing [sic] year better than the past which we purpose to do if Almighty God deliver us from our present dreadful situation."*
> —*the diary of Patrick Breen, December 31, 1846*

Knowing you were waiting
on the other side of it,
                                    my train
cut through the thickly-sliced fat
of snow
              to the bone. The wheels sang
my love is good my love is good.
                                    And then, nothing.

—

and then, a boulder. And then
we were pinned
                        to the tracks. We were honest:
we were the sort of folks
who'd believe a man when he said
                                          shortcut
without ever having taken it himself.

—

hearts go bad
          like something on a shelf
that's all. Your letter, a letter
                        with paragraphs in it, being packed.

—

4

We couldn't move
                    if we wanted to,
so we call disaster
                    by its married name:
a setback, a small delay—

—

I forgive you.
You, who have so much
to be forgiven for.
                    The universe
is a graceless one. Who killed them
                                        but their own,
and where did they go
                    with all of the choicest cuts?

After Time Has Rumpled the Sheets of Your Mouth

When I am winter, shutting privately down in my own deep snow,
allow me solace in stinking rooms of books, typewriters cold and dressed
for procession. Great old ghosts grousing on stairwells, tumblers in cuff

and not a kind word on their paper lips. Allow me mercy in my frozen
thicket, where parties will have come to call and left to hibernate, leaving
behind small tracks of silent pears, tepid angels in wakeful repose.

& allow me comforts—sliced membrillo, an avocado churned by spoon,
port in crystal tasting of exquisite girls, black cherries, a photograph
smoldering magenta. Leave me hopeful for another. Waiter! *Another.*

To the Larks, Who Know Nothing of What We Do
For Charlotte Mew

I cannot tell a lie, and so—

In truth, we came after, and thus it was easier.

In truth, my thumbs press the grass.

In truth, you are buried under the grass, and it has grown over you.

In truth, there is no grave at all.

In truth, this is a poem, what I am touching is truth: a frogging artery.

In truth, you search for larks from the grave of your poem.

(In truth, you never got to love a woman)

In truth, this is the end of all roads.

In truth, the birds are women. In truth, the grass is women.

In truth, the bicep, the body, the grave—women.
In truth, I have loved many. I have loved none.

Ars Poetica

One would like to see oneself walking through the forest as two girls,
    along a creek, golden carp under the ice like blurred poppies.
The tall, hooded girl will extend a basket, offering bread and water, a kindly
    face and a thick cloak.
The other is small, with sly hands. She will eat her fill, wrap herself
    in the warmth of the wool cloak, cut a branch from a tree.
Whittling the end to a point, she will pull the arrow back, and shoot it
    into the throat of the hooded girl. She will retrieve the basket.

Intolerable Objects: Tomato

The first was sliced thick, watery and viscous
with seedy mire, menses on Irish thighs.

Arizona, immaculate kitchen window
a picture show with a poodle skirt of cumulous.

Lettuce, now gored into an irreparable fen, lies
complicit on a plate, smells of clammy nightshades.

Once I was a hothouse gone to seed,
that tract apartment outside of Buckeye,

vermillion in skillful ataraxia, no cultivation.
Clock hands welt afternoon into pulpy

slaughter, into bright silver and cresting
to sick aubergine, dinner table the color of a beetle

preserved in sap. When merciful troops
of aphids arrive, steady in the night, I heave

the bosom of scarlet filth from dishware
to toilet drain, the blood pools.

In the yard, a woman paid to care
feeds our soiled underwear to potbelly pigs.

Alternative Bedtime Story

She opens her mouth.

In this story, the child makes a house out of a box,
a river from a pile of dead leaves,
a companion from a cloud formation,
and a self of shifting ponds.
Her parents are lost in the fog
on a train somewhere in the mountains,
and when she sleeps, she slumbers well.

There is a word for adopted children,
they are called *fawns*. The woods are full of them,
and their biggest adversary is the night,
and the owls who call to mice as they shrink away,
and large sequoias who light themselves on sacrifice.

In a story she dreams at home in a bed.
A child makes a home in a soft trunk
in a clearing of sword ferns. It is full
of fat worms and sleeping possums,
and the stars are stored away somewhere,
spinning and sparking against each other.
And when they die, she knows nothing of it.

Saguaros

Arizona rises in welts.

It pinches New Mexico and my mother,
the menstruating horizon between the two.

Thus it was with her. She, a cloud long
and placed perfectly. Sky strong and full
of torn cornflower blue, ravaged
to strings. Before me, the babies were born
as still and silent as mercury. A victory
to her when her field caught seed
and bloomed startlingly open—

I was born in a dry world, and we lived
as chasms among men, saguaros
with hundreds of years holding rain;
the same, in a sense
as wild beasts in battle, who want for water.

We were mistaken in taking
from the cracked ground, brown
and spent. Forget men.
We were better off withholding.

I tell you this because she's gone, now,
and you are a kind and forgiving reader,
seeking truth.

For truth, I say I remember
this mother, the mother of my nights
bringing home a jackrabbit,
pulling a tooth trap from its pelage to slit
the pregnant belly, knowing
the body to be a stasis and the desert a hell,
and the knife the only bridge between the two.

II. Millions, Myriads

"We waited, either forgetting what we were
or becoming more brightly human in that pine"

—Katie Ford, *November Philosophers*

V. Woolf Rewrites History

I said the words the best I could.
I dreamt, upon her death, a door.
To think she was on the other side!
I could have opened, and crossed
the threshold as a bride, and now I never shall.

The Dirty War
Buenos Aires, Argentina 1976

Evenings we dance the wooden room
down to splinters, last jar of bathtub wine,
dancing we drink it in San Telmo's pixelated
throat, all saints alive and stretching themselves
over cab drivers, drunks, and travellers.
We make air for ourselves by exhaling to ash
and birch, the body bows a feint over Plaza de Mayo,
mothers of disappeared boys, soldiers in hollow,
take my arms. The grass feigns milonga. We dance.

Evenings we dance open doors of men
writing plays of lady Eva, stars still bubbling
in hidden tango joints under streets, we dance you,
puppeting and pulling strangers from kiosks
of empanadas. The gentle movement of groins
in resentful sync is enough to make a city weep—
Corpus Christi flocks today in a head of triangular
birds, and now the air is full of wet paper. We dance.

Evenings we drink to you from balconies
littered in utility bills, love gained, danced, drunk,
vomited before mid-morning. We dance cigars
into molting slag, into timepieces for conversation,
into pity: sir driver, you used to be a saint?
We dance for you, for the lights refusing
their green, the mothers refusing communion,
the Plaza refusing new fountains until old boys bloom,
emerging from women's embroidered scarves.

Chopin's Funeral March

Grandmother's mouth vowels the air. The mother
is not underwater, but under soil. No one surfaces
from under stones but the mother's daughter, an heir
to the living poke-grass and fresh dirt.

Not underwater but under soil. No one surfaces
except through hymns, and the day takes back
the living poke-grass and fresh dirt.
Sleep croons a peaty and unpleasant note

and except through hymns, when the day takes back
the phone, as it did what it was asked, dialing 9-1-1-1-1-1—
sleep croons a peaty and unpleasant note.
like a moth the granddaughter swallowed, knowing nothing.

The mother has no point of view. She's dead.
The grandmother's mouth vowels air, above a mother
cold in January rain, cold in her bed
under stones and the mother's daughter, an heir.

If V. Woolf Had Printed Ulysses

The page feeds through a long sheet
of cream slightly dappled, almost curdled.

It grinds through the press like a catcall,
gears turning the slicked letters over reams—

Stately, plump buck Mulligan seeming
stately. Plump. She turns the crank again

pedal pumping paper at her left hand
so quickly the words blur and flee.

Were it her Clarissa, the perfect host,
the papers would not fly so fast

through the press's carriage, arrested
in their movement, their frenzied rouse.

How different, the poverty of her sex.
Joyce, in his allowances, just broke a wall.

Pinochet Speaks From His Casket
December 10th, 2006

There was a strike. That much was obvious.

Papers in the air, those bright burnt birds.

And somewhere, a young face—I know it not,
came into my dead, blurred vision, staying a spell,
waving a grenade, biting into it as if
a pomegranate. And when I chanced

to meet his eye, he strayed to the stars
on my breast, my decorated bronze
and golden leaves—and why
was I in such a small box, such a sheath
to hold a sword this size? I see only half
the world from here, the sky a processional
I never asked for: quiet, oppressive.

When my boy Osvaldo was young and fearful
of dreadful lightning that struck the field,
the terrible cracking of thunder, like a sheet
pulled crisp over a cold bed—I, too,
pulled him into my arms, said *We are not large enough
to be harmed*, while the wind toughened around us.
My boy, my boy, named for me, howled.
And looked, when I thought of it, like burnt wheat.

The young man with the grenade speaks, crying
a call and response that others join. A boy once.

He has died, he said.

I've died? I think.

My window quickly fills with heavy rain,
mucous and spit, and all my boys
clutch newsprint emblazed with my face.
Not a leaf moves in this country without me knowing—

On the Death of Thomas Kinkade

Confession.

The relationship was of an intimate
nature, thighs blushing in shapes

like cottage bricks, end
of an imperfect virtue, let alone *day*!

Wind mills turning up blade skies
like tilled butter, and after all that sin,

seven days, on the fourth, the suave
stroked lapels of a free clinic,

morning a drop in a creased white coat.

Now.

Light funnels through the room,
speculum throne bowing in grace,

with stirrup wings—antiseptic cathedral
of sea salt and floor cleaner, forced

light body lithe, saturated pastels
in water: dental dams, free prophylactics

in five-and-dime shapes, His hands
anoint themselves in a basin, thick

drops of lemon are rubbed on chalky fingers
and tongue depressors wave from their stations,

Thomas staring down from high
above examining rooms, prostrate.

V. Woolf at the Corner Market

Eggs in plastic bags, dammit to hell.
Flowers, yes, in brown paper, no doubt, no doubt
at all. Ducking here, between the watermelons
with their kiss-lips in the air, she ducks here
behind the apples, sees Vita, a dream with bread.
She wants to tuck a white tulip in her wide lapel,
paint her cheeks with the watermelon's last sigh
of summer, to want. To want.

She drops the eggs. Maybe in their last seconds
of flight they remember the farm—the velvet beds
of their mothers, the scratching of brothers and sisters
inside their shells. They smash against the ground,
like noisy yellow protests in the spice aisle,
all for nothing, showing she's here.

Freud Looking at a Picture of His Mother

Move the photo closer,
that I might see the look
of discontent. A skeletal sky
dressed in funeral colors. Does Vienna
play chess in the background?
O, joy, mother, these trees
grow pure bombs in the fall,
and by October, we can fill
our mouths with grit.
Don't ask me why my descent
was silent, why I never looked
into the face of hell as I climbed down
your name. The heat below the Earth
was cooler to the touch
than developers' chemicals.
It sustained me. As I thought of you,
my arms ceased their function.
The night is still now. The mice
hold court in the kitchen, skittering your name.
Hell turns itself over and empties into the world.

If V. Woolf filled her pockets with balloons instead of rocks

Wires below are cutting land into property.
From above, the houses look like small, blockish heads,
chimney-mouths in surprised Os, long blurs of green fields
and strange silo shapes. Leonard will be sleeping,
dreaming of the kettle's steam. And then the clouds
come up suddenly, shocking in large elephants of white hair,
faces unimpressed with your buoyed body, careful bun.
Go back to your man, your drawer full of letters, one softer cloud
motions. *Stop being a fool with balloons.* At once, you hit your head
on a black bit of plastic. You rattle the sky and stars.
The clouds tsk you, gathering together like a bouquet of black peonies.
You have reached the edge of the set, and there is nowhere else to go.

Additional Acknowledgements

This manuscript would not be possible without the help of a vast community of generously-spirited people. To name a few: Pamela Petro, Kevin Prufer, Sharon Bryan, Eve Linn, AC Panella, Stephanie Glazier, Kamala Puligandla, Maurice Manning, Jean Valentine, J. Ratliff, and the Oakland contingent of the Bay Area literary community. I am also grateful for the support of the Dickinson House, the Vermont Studio Center, Sewanee, and the Lambda Literary Foundation.

July Westhale is a poet and essayist living in Oakland, CA. She has been awarded grants and residencies from the Vermont Studio Center, the Lambda Literary Foundation, Sewanee, Tomales Bay, Dickinson House, Tin House and Bread Loaf. *The Cavalcade* is her debut collection. www.julywesthale.com.

www.ingramcontent.com/pod-product-compliance
Lightning Source LLC
LaVergne TN
LVHW041329080426
835513LV00008B/657